AVOIDING ANOTHER GREAT DEPRESSION

AVOIDING ANOTHER GREAT DEPRESSION

Written By

SALEEM SHAIKH

E-mail:avoidthedepression@gmail.com
Avoiding Another Great Depression 1st Edition

Publication Date: March 2021
Price: ₹250 | $ 10.00
ISBN: 978-93-90566-50-1
Published by:
Adhyyan Books
Office No. 125,
Opposite Vivanta by Taj,
DDA SFS. Pocket-1, Dwarka,
Sec-22, New Delhi-110077
Website: http://adhyyanbooks.com
E-mail: contact@adhyyanbooks.com

ABOUT THE BOOK

This book presents my unconventional, controversial and revolutionary point of view for addressing the economic tsunami being unleashed in the aftermath of the pandemic. Suggesting policies and actions to be put in place to avoid another great depression.
I may not have the power to change the world on my own, but I can stir the pot, and this book is my attempt to do so.

- *The Author*

To my son Ashbaan who is
the fountainhead of all the
inspiration in my life.

CONTENTS

1
Synopsis

This booklet aims to review the problem of the on-going pandemic and proposes a framework of measures and mechanisms to minimize and avoid a great depression scenario resulting from the on-going pandemic. It not only attempts to suggest 'what to do' but also 'how to do' and 'who does what' by identifying roles and responsibilities in addressing the gigantic problem of the impending economic tsunami resulting from the pandemic. The focus of this booklet is global in nature as it does not concentrate on a specific nation as such, but proposes measures and mechanisms in general that are applicable more or less to all the affected nations. Each individual nation can pick up on these and work out the specifics tailored for their national economies, resources at hand and national priorities.

2
Understanding The Problem

The on-going pandemic has virtually engulfed almost all of humanity. It all started seemingly towards the end of the year 2019. At the time of this writing, the virus was known to have infected about 125 million people (perhaps many more as testing is limited across the globe and many cases are undetected), killed nearly 3 million, and infecting at the rate of about half a million additional people a day (again probably many more).

In addition to these human casualties, the pandemic has also cost millions of lost jobs, millions of businesses closing down, trillions of dollars wiped out of the global economy, and the devastation continues unabated.

As the pandemic is still in its infancy (just a few months old), the major focus currently is more on the healthcare aspect of the pandemic with major emphasis and resources being prioritised and devoted for testing, detection, protection, care, developing quarantine centres, rehabilitation, developing vaccines, damage control, etc.

In addition to the healthcare tsunami unleashed by the virus, the economic impact of the pandemic has also begun to unravel and snowballing as we speak. And what a catastrophe this is turning out to be. When the pandemic becomes less of an issue, the debts and economic destruction unleashed by it will play havoc on all of humanity.

> *COVID-19 is likely to persist once its pandemic phase has passed and circulate each winter alongside the flu. Even after more of us contract coronavirus infection and develop immunity to it or even after an effective vaccine arrives, some people will still get very sick.*
> *- Scott Gottlieb*

While the picture still seems to be a bit blurred about the economic impact of the pandemic, the world is certainly heading towards a great depression scenario unless unprecedented, unconventional, drastic and previously unimaginable measures are taken on a war footing, as a top priority and on a global scale.

3
Some Predictions

Before proceeding further, I thought it prudent to document what I foresee in the near future as consequences of this pandemic. We as humanity are facing the combined equivalent of the Spanish flue of the 1918-1920 and the great depression of the 1930's at the same time and on an even larger scale. I do foresee the following developments in the near future and wish to be proved wrong on many of them:

The global GDP wipe out could well be $10-15 trillion in 2020, around $10 trillion in 2021, and $5-10 trillion in 2022 and in 2023. And this could be the best case scenario as I expect the wipe out to continue for a few more years to 2030 albeit at gradually diminishing magnitude.

The intangible losses would additionally amount to more trillions as well (erosion of real estate valuations globally for example).

I do not see the global economy returning to pre pandemic levels before 2025 at best. Perhaps for 10 years leading up to the year 2030 would be a cautious optimism.

Government deficits worldwide could amount to over $10 trillion in 2020.

IMF sees world economy shrinking by 4.9% in 2020. I see it shrinking by 10% at least.

The days of the US dollar domination in the global economy are going to end. The days of the US dollar as a global reserve currency are numbered. The dollar will lose value against major currencies. The collapse of the US dollar is imminent.

Gold will gain in prominence as a safe haven for investors.

Digital currencies will gain prominence among the young generation and witness significant growth in valuations albeit gradually.

Within the next five to six years, China will surpass the US as the world's largest economy in US$ terms.

I expect sovereign defaults by at least 10-15 nations during the period from 1st Jan 2020 to 31st Dec 2021 and that will include at least one, perhaps two, may be up to 4 major economies (from among the world's top 20 economies that constitute almost 80% of the global economy). And those are conservative estimates.

Among the major economies, I expect China to be the least affected by the pandemic, perhaps managing to stay in positive territory despite the pandemic (Its GDP will grow instead of contracting though at a lesser rate than pre pandemic levels).

Nations of the orient such as South Korea, Japan, Taiwan, Hong Kong, China as well as Vietnam, should be able to recover faster and will witness lesser damage to their respective economies from the pandemic.

There will be a paradigm shift in the way we live, work and conduct business. Nations will increasingly witness migration to digital platforms from physical interactions. WFM (work from home) models will gain preference over working from offices. People will move out from city centres and business hubs to city outskirts and suburbs that offer less rental and real estate costs. Likewise, migration from cities & urban hotspots to villages, rural areas and country sides will increase. There will also be a paradigm shift in the travel patterns. In these pandemic times, people are commuting less, avoiding long distance travels, traveling shorter distances, minimizing means of public and mass transport and are increasingly resorting to bikes, cycles and scooters for shorter runs, social distancing and cost savings. Did someone say bullock carts, horse rides, chariots and carriages? Not yet I guess.

The urban population hotspots will witness an easing of population densities, erosion in real estate valuations and diminishing rental yields.

Worldwide there will be a spike in migration of people to countries and regions perceived to be safer in the foreseeable future in terms of the emerging scenario.

I foresee a decrease in life expectancy as a direct consequence of the pandemic. The patterns emerging over the last few months suggest that the effects of the virus are more pronounced among the elderly as well as those with co morbidities. Moreover it has also been found that those who have recovered still have health implications in varying degrees, with the worst hit being those who recovered after they had to be put on ventilators. Nations with more of an ageing population and already less life expectancy may be the worst hit in this regards.

As nations feel the pinch of economic recession/depression, the system of barter of goods will gain traction. Even digital currencies will gain in popularity. The importance of fiat money and currencies may diminish.

The relative exchange rates between currencies will see major ups and downs and there will be a total overhaul of exchange rates with new and surprising equations emerging in currency exchange rates.

Non-essential and luxury items such as designer products, apparels, electronics, furniture, consumer durables, high end automobiles, real estate, holiday travel, tourism, will take significant hit.

Nations with tourism as the main source of income will suffer significantly on the economic front as tourism will be worst hit under the shadow of the pandemic.

With the approaching change in season and the onset of winters, a second wave of the virus is probably lined up on the horizon.

The pandemic will give rise to an unprecedented world food crisis affecting at least an additional 200 million souls globally. The world will witness significant increase in hunger and poverty.

True individual freedom cannot exist without economic security and independence. People who are hungry and out of a job are the stuff of which dictatorships are made.
- Franklin D. Roosevelt

Given the prevailing gender bias, misogyny and patriarchy in many societies, women will be more affected by the food crisis and resulting consequences such as malnutrition as compared to men. Being perceived as the weaker sex, they may find themselves subjected to increased violence, abuse and crimes against women.

Unless there is recognition that women are most vulnerable... and you do something about social and cultural equality for women, you're never going to defeat this pandemic.
- Stephen Lewis

Infant mortality rates will increase as malnourished women achieve motherhood on the one hand and increased poverty and reduced incomes will limit childcare on the other hand.

The gap between the rich and the poor will increase. Social unrest, riots, looting, violence and lawlessness will increase. Many flash points of conflicts will sprout across the globe.

Job losses could well be in the range of 200-300 million globally as employers across the spectrum continue to reduce the human resources at all levels (organized, unorganized sectors, Small and Medium Businesses, entrepreneurs, etc.).

Nations globally will witness a rise of the Gig economy. Gig economy refers to a free market system in which traditional businesses hire independent contractors, freelancers, and short-term workers to perform individual tasks, assignments, or jobs in preference to full time permanent employees.

The banking industry globally is all set to struggle with unprecedented loan defaults and mounting NPA's on the one hand and diminishing credit off take on the other.

The banking industry globally will have to write off bad debts like never before.

Expect stock market crashes and corrections in coming months as disappointing economies, and diminishing fiscal support across the world leads to gradually reducing demand, price cuts and wafer thin margins significantly impacting returns and valuations across the board.

Businesses will increasingly embrace e-commerce and move online. Retail, FMCG, consumer electronics, home appliances, groceries, apparel, and even professional services will increasingly move online. Work from home (WFH) will be the new normal in many sectors. IT consultancy and infrastructure companies providing ecommerce solutions and the enabling technology and platforms for this transition will flourish around the world.

4
The Three Stages of The Problem

Let us try to understand the three stages of the entire problem:

Stage 1: The Virus Spread

This is the initial stage in which the virus first spreads in the society which is the epicentre and eventually engulfs the entire nation, spills beyond its borders and subsequently spreads far and wide virtually covering all of humanity. Infections continue to grow and engulf more and more of the population, wreaking havoc on the societies. The world has already witnessed this stage and is reeling in its aftermath. This stage is characterized by panic, chaos, nervousness and the likes both among the general population, medical fraternity as well as the governance.

Stage 2: The Vaccination

In this stage efforts at creating a vaccine, antidote or cure are undertaken and once these have materialized, a global effort of vaccinating the population is undertaken. The virus still continues to spread albeit at a lesser rate as most of the infected population has achieved immunity. The economic effects of the pandemic start becoming evident and efforts at addressing them have begun as well.

Stage 3: Fixing The Economy

In this stage the economic devastation unleashed by the pandemic becomes clear and focus shifts to fixing the economy as the rate of spread of the virus subsides and the availability of a vaccine instils confidence among the masses. The panic, chaos and nervousness evaporates from the society and efforts are streamlined towards rebuilding the economy, restoring businesses, creating jobs, infusing financial stimulus and the likes. This is the longest stage on the timeline of the problem as economic devastation in the aftermath of the pandemic takes a long while to get economies back on track.

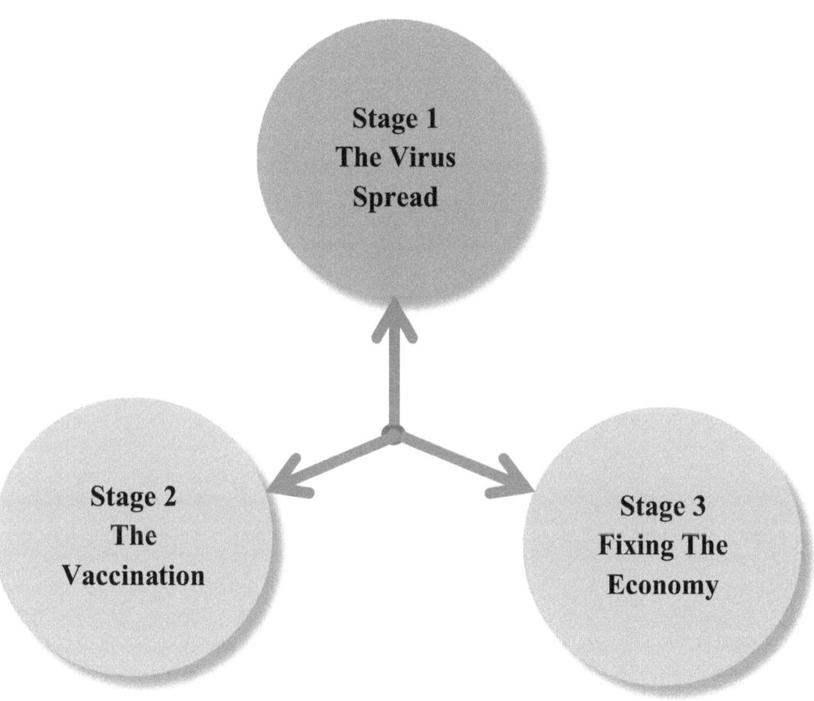

Figure 1: The Three Stages of The Problem

In my opinion the three stages will last about a decade before full normalcy, especially on the economic front, is restored. Following is an approximate depiction of my anticipated timelines:

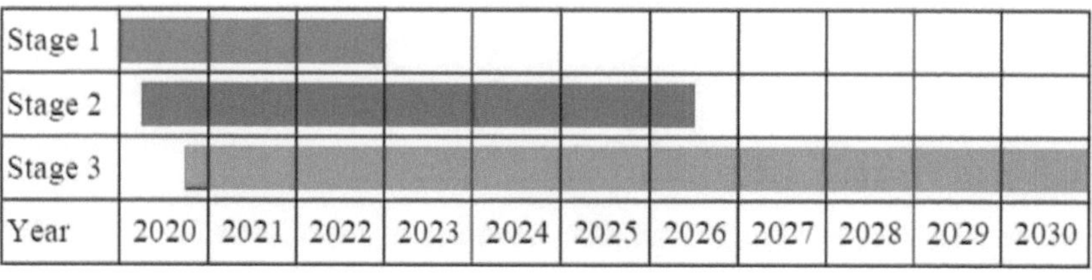

Figure 2: Timeline – The Three Stages of The Problem

5
What Can Be Done?

Well, proposing solutions for tackling such a global phenomenon as this pandemic is no mean task. However this booklet attempts to discuss various measures, actions, strategies that can be adopted by the global community in fighting the pandemic and minimizing the healthcare and economic impact of the pandemic.

The Pre Requisites:

The world has to acknowledge that this pandemic is a severe global phenomenon engulfing all nations and threatening to destabilize the global economy. It's already becoming the major disaster that humanity has faced since the world war – II and the most catastrophic impact on the global economy since the great depression of the 1930's. It has to be understood and drilled into our minds that solutions to such a problem of global scale cannot be conventional. Conventional thinking and wisdom will have to take the back seat as bold, risky, unprecedented, out of the box thinking and never before actions and decisions are required to confront this situation and prevail.

> *The dogmas of the quiet past are inadequate to the stormy present. The occasion is piled high with difficulty, and we must rise with the occasion. As our case is new, so we must think anew and act anew.*
> *- Abraham Lincoln*

World leaders, global institutions, governments and citizens will have to make sacrifices, put their politics, ego's, arrogance, ideologies, greed, ambitions, disputes and differences aside and work with sincere efforts to confront the situation.

> *The only thing more dangerous than ignorance is arrogance.*
> *- Albert Einstein*

Mutual cooperation is the need of the hour. We all need each other's help and will have to work as one cohesive, monolithic humanity at this time. It is clearer than ever that none of us will be safe until all of us are safe.

> *Coronavirus anywhere is a threat to people everywhere.*
> *- Ellen Johnson Sirleaf, Former Liberian President*

The world will take years to return to pre pandemic levels. In the interim, days of sacrifices, shunning materialism, avoiding luxuries, indulging in hard work, diminished expectations, modest lifestyles, etc. have to be endured by all if we have to reduce the sufferings and damage and come out of this situation. Modest life style has to be the new normal.

> *The world has enough for everyone's needs, but not for everyone's greed.*
> *- Mahatma Gandhi*

The Three Pronged Strategy:

By and large, the efforts needed, boil down to three main categories:

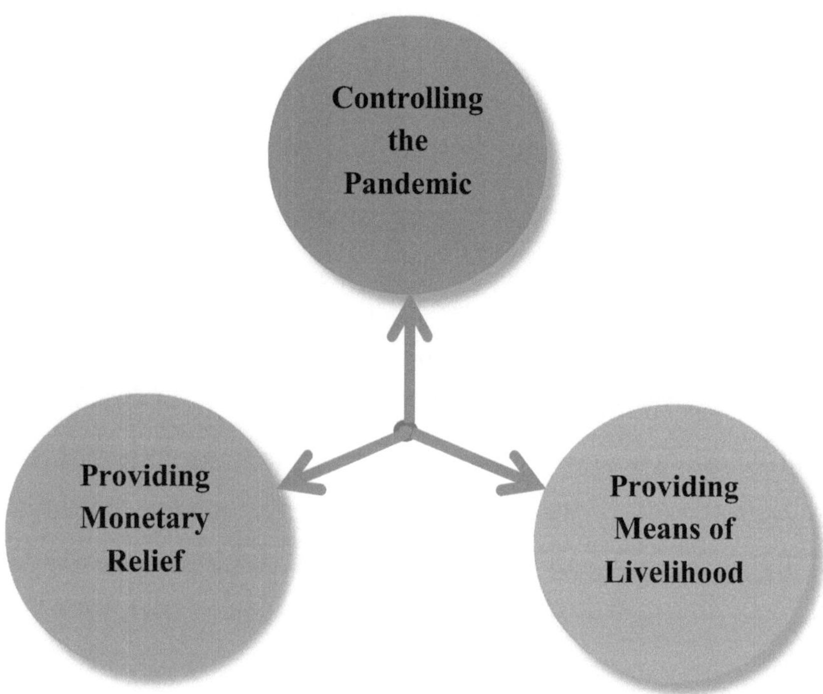

Figure 3 - The Three Pronged Strategy

This probably doesn't need explaining. The entire action plan discussed in this text is aimed at addressing these three fundamentals.

Controlling the Pandemic:

Budget allocations, efforts, human resources, research, health care infrastructure, immunization programs, etc. required to minimize, control, and contain the pandemic will have to be given top priority.

Providing Monetary Relief:

As people lose jobs and livelihoods, MSME's (Micro, Small and Medium Enterprises) struggle for survival and economics are jammed worldwide, nations will have to undertake massive relief efforts in the form of monetary assistance and cash injections.

Providing Means of Livelihood:

Nations will have to take measures to ensure their citizens have means of livelihood and are able to sustain themselves during this crisis and enterprises are able to survive through the pandemic. This will keep the economies ticking.

The Responsibility Pyramid:

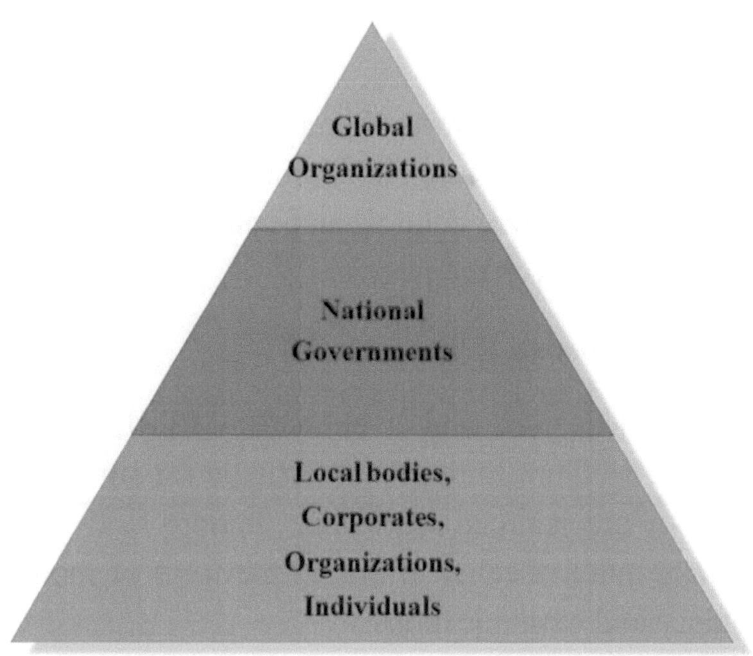

Figure 4 – The Responsibility Pyramid

The responsibility for implementing the action plan proposed in this text starts with global organizations and boils down to every single individual.

Global Organizations:

These include the United Nations (UN), the International Monetary Fund (IMF), the World Health Organization (WHO), the World Trade Organization (WTO) and the World Bank.

National Governments:

Federal governments and monarchies of individual nations have a key role to play in framing policies both, within their nation as well as their foreign policies aimed at achieving the common goal of addressing the problem at hand.

Local Institutions & Individuals:

These include provincial/state governments, various organizations, NGO's, corporate entities, and individual citizens.

It has to be absorbed by all concerned that bold and unconventional decisions will have to be made based on prevailing facts and circumstances rather than toying the line of conventional wisdom deployed in normal situations and circumstances.

Sacrifices have to be made by all concerned; nations, governments, organizations, corporates, businesses as well as individuals if we have to come out of this with the minimum possible damage to citizens and economies. The intentions and mentality of making money and profiteering out of this disaster has to be arrested and neutralized. There has to be a paradigm shift like never before. Modest life style has to be the new normal for quite some time from now on.

> *Great achievement is usually born out of great sacrifice and is never the result of selfishness.*
> *- Napoleon Hill*

6
The Role of Global Organizations

To tackle this global threat, the rich nations need to support the developing countries. Writing off their debt (partially or fully) and/or restructuring the same and helping them build comprehensive healthcare is the need of the hour. Global organizations can play a vital role in promoting and coordinating such debt write offs and other healthcare assistance that can be provided to the affected developing nations.

The IMF and WHO will have to work in tandem with various nations to ensure large scale coordinated production and distribution of the vaccine worldwide, when available, in the shortest possible time and at affordable price points. This is not going to be a mean task. These organizations in coordination with various governments will have to fund (partly or fully, an IMF action item) and undertake mass vaccination programs on a global level. The challenges faced will be royalties and patent rights by vaccine developers on the one hand and the rich nations grabbing the vaccine stocks before it becomes available to other nations on the other hand. It has to be understood that an uptick in global economic activity is directly related to reduced infections and control of the virus.

The COVAX initiative co-led by the Coalition for Epidemic Preparedness Innovations (CEPI), the Gavi vaccine alliance, and the WHO is one significant step aimed at ensuring equitable access to COVID-19 vaccines across the world, once the vaccines are licensed and approved. However at the time of this writing, the process of garnering the support of nations to this initiative and getting them on board was underway. Moreover the initiative will also have to establish supply chains and distribution networks for its intended aim of reaching out and delivering the vaccine to the neediest on a priority. It will have to struggle through its shortcomings and limitations in deterring rich nations from laying their hands on (grabbing) the vaccine before anyone else.

Large scale testing for the virus, preventive and protective measures, treatment and rehabilitation of the affected, spreading education and awareness about the COVID-19 virus, etc. will continue to be a health sector priority for the next 4 to 5 years and the WHO will have to continue to play a leading role in facilitating and monitoring this along with various national governments.

Any and all kinds of sanctions shall be outlawed. The UN must ensure that either such sanctions are lifted by the nations and/or organizations that have imposed them or over ruled and outlawed (International Court of Justice which is the principal judicial organ of the UN can come into play if required to ensure that all sanctions are outlawed). This is not the time for sanctions which at often times are discriminatory and serve the political interests of nations imposing them.

There is a need to establish trading blocs with duty free trading and even barter system between neighbouring nations sharing common boundaries, cultures and goals. This also can be explored by already established groups of nations catering to common agenda's. Existing groups of nations such as G-20, SAARC, BRICS, OIC, EU, ASEAN, GCC, etc. are examples. More such arrangements can emerge. Such duty free trading arrangements between members of a group of nations will promote trade and commerce with mutual benefits helping their economies to recover. This is obviously a WTO action item in coordination with such groups and individual nations.

The UN must ensure global peace and work to pre-empt and avoid conflicts and potential flash points. This will help individual nations to reduce defence spending (which forms a significant component of any government spending) and divert the resulting savings towards battling the pandemic and its economic impact. Maintaining global peace in these difficult times is the need of the hour.

7
The Role of National Governments

Governments have to understand that universal basic income is the need of the hour. The world has to understand that lack of basic needs is forcing millions to struggle and toil full time in achieving the same, when they could have contributed those energies, skills and time to something more meaningful for the society. All nations without exceptions must adopt a universal basic income regime. This can perhaps be the most efficient tool in providing relief to all affected citizens.

To tackle the global threat of a looming depression, the rich nations need to support the developing countries. Writing off their debt (partially or fully) and/or restructuring the same will ease the economic burden on these affected nations. The rich nations can also help support the developing nations by helping them build comprehensive healthcare.

The world must address the issue of unequal distribution of wealth and address it NOW. A more equitable wealth distribution is the need of the hour.

> *Without equity, pandemic battles will fail. Viruses will simply recirculate, and perhaps undergo mutations or changes that render vaccines useless, passing through the unprotected populations of the planet.*
> *- Laurie Garrett*

Nations must Tax the rich over and above the current levels. The world's richest 1% possesses twice the wealth of the rest of humanity combined. At the time of this writing, the top 12 billionaires in the USA collectively owned over a trillion dollars of wealth. Let that sink in.

> *Governments are massively under-taxing the rich individuals and corporations, and under-funding public services.*
> *- Oxfam*

A maximum wealth cap of $1-2 billion by an individual should make sense going forwards. The rest of the individual wealth shall be given back to the nation. No human being at any place on earth needs more than a billion for his entire life, means of livelihood, raising a family, financial security and what have you. Humanity in its present time simply cannot sustain the huge wealth gap between the rich and the poor.

> *Our broken economies are lining the pockets of billionaires and big businesses at the expense of ordinary men and women. No wonder people are starting to question whether billionaires should even exist.*
> *- Amitabh Behar, Oxfam India CEO*

Those with incomes of more than a million dollars per annum shall be taxed at least 50% and those above 10 million dollars in annual income shall be taxed 75%.

> *The test of our progress is not whether we add more to the abundance of those who have much; it is whether we provide enough for those who have little.*
> *- Franklin D. Roosevelt*

All nations without exceptions must implement a Land Ceiling Act that defines the maximum area of land that an individual is allowed to own. This ceiling can be categorized into urban/non-agricultural land and agricultural land for obvious reasons. Land is a fixed resource and a more equitable distribution of the same is the need of our times.

Nations must improve the tax collection systems by increasingly adopting Information Technology tools and platforms, centralizing data & information, minimizing pilferage and strengthening deterrence for violators.

More effective fraud, bribery, kick-backs and corruption control measures are the need of the hour to save every penny for priority spending. National governments will have to jack up the resources for the same.

Population control measures are a necessity going forwards. Nations without exceptions must adopt and facilitate family planning measures. A two child policy should be the norm. The rich and advanced nations where population issues are not as pronounced as some of the impoverished nations, can help the more affected nations in this regards.

Universal and affordable healthcare is the need of our times. All nations with whatever means available at their disposal shall implement a universal healthcare program that provides healthcare for all its citizens. While healthcare initiatives are prevalent in many countries most of them need to be reformed to effectively serve the intended purpose.

Nations with well-developed medical infrastructure and less affected by the virus can provide health care professionals to nations that have weak health care systems, and worst affected by the pandemic. A global movement of healthcare professionals across borders is inevitable in containing the virus.

Nations must draft final year medical college and nursing students into full-time/part-time health care services to plug-in the shortfall of medical professionals. COVID-19 related healthcare does not involve complex surgeries and procedures and final year students can assist in the same. Their contribution can be recognized and rewarded by including their service period as part of their academic tenure or internships or by some other suitable means.

Healthcare spending in the short term, shall prioritize on COVID-19 related care, rehabilitation, vaccine development, acquiring health care professionals, creating healthcare facilities to accommodate the infection loads in the population, increasing awareness, etc.

There will be a spike in the use of internet and means of mobile communications for doing business, providing services, work from home (WFH) initiatives, education, video conferencing, etc. Nations will have to significantly scale up their online infrastructure to meet these demands.

Automation in manufacturing will reduce physical interactions and contacts in these pandemic times. Similarly deploying equipment and robotic technologies to reduce human involvement in physical aspects is the need of the hour to help contain the virus.

The need to maintain peace, justice, law and order in society by respective governments will be a daunting task and a pre requisite to addressing the challenges on the economic front as well as in controlling the epidemic.

Nations must ensure that budget allocations are meant for the highest of priorities in these difficult times. Non-essential projects and spending can wait for the time being. Control of unjustified expenses have to be put in place with better approval regimes and checks and balances at various levels.

National governments globally may have to rewrite budgets with re allocations attuned with the pandemic related challenges at hand. Upcoming budgets for the next 3-5 years will have to accommodate the new challenges. Spending on luxuries, defence, and certain elements of public infrastructure will have to take the back seat.

> *The trade deficit always goes up when the economy is strong and plummets when the economy sinks, as it did during both the Great Depression of the 1930s and the Great Recession of 2008-09.*
> *- Stephen Moore*

Nations will have to restructure debts (national debt, corporate sector debts - both public and private - and individual debts). This may be necessitated in order to provide a breather to the borrowers on the one hand and save the pile up of NPA's with the banks on the other.

Nations will be confronted with the daunting task of reduced revenues on the one hand and increased spending for fiscal support on the other. There is a need to balance relief, stimulus and health care spending with reduced tax revenues. Governments across the world will struggle to balance reduced revenues against unprecedented stimulus. Going by conventional wisdom, closing fiscal deficit will require significant increase in tax revenues and a significant decrease in public spending. However taxes cannot be increased under the current scenario for the common man or the MSMB's (Micro, Small and Medium Businesses and Enterprises). Conventional fiscal deficit considerations will have to be put on the back burner for the time being.

Fiscal measures pertaining to the COVID-19 crisis shall be in the region of 10-15% of global GDP varying from 10 to 30% of a nation's GDP depending on severity of the crisis. The fiscal stimulus shall focus mainly on stimulating the economic recovery.

Government disinvestments and monetizing of state assets such as land, properties, state owned enterprises, share holdings, etc. can generate substantial funds to support economic recovery. Government can also put to good use its reserves in these times of crisis. If the conventional fiscal deficit considerations are still on the table, these measures of disinvestments will help check the fiscal deficit. Family Silver comes to the rescue during times of crisis, isn't it?

In the early phase of the pandemic, the focus has to be on saving lives, providing relief, containing the virus, developing vaccines and treatments, rehabilitation, and the likes. In the second phase, which shall partially overlap the first, the focus has to shift towards addressing the gigantic economic fallout and consequences of the pandemic such as saving jobs, businesses, industries, financial institutions, etc.

Nations will be engaged in saving lives and livelihoods by putting money in the hands of the people, undertaking unprecedented job creation programs, and increased healthcare spending.

Relief and stimulus packages to be periodically undertaken with the main focus being households and MSMB's (Micro, Small and Medium Businesses and Enterprises).

Nations can undertake more and more PPP (Public Private Partnership) projects to reduce the burden on the national budget.

A promotion of modest life style and giving up on luxurious living shall be promoted through role models, social media influencers, celebrities, sports icons and the likes.

Major world economies will have to shape up to significantly lower levels of spending than what existed in the pre-COVID era.

Defence spending which forms a significant component of government spending by many nations globally can be minimized by ensuring peace prevails in the global community during these difficult times. Defence spending will have to be drastically reduced globally by all concerned nations. The resulting savings can contribute to reducing fiscal deficits and help nations to spend on greater priorities at hand in the wake of the pandemic. That places a greater responsibility on the UN and individual nations to ensure global peace and work to pre-empt and avoid conflicts and potential flash points.

Corporate taxes around the globe must be reduced to a maximum of 15% in the interim. Existing levels lower than 15% may be retained.

All nations must reduce GST, VAT, sales tax and similar taxes and duties on products and services. Property registration charges, stamp duties, etc. must also be reduced/waived off for at least a couple of years. These measures will help prop up sales and consumption of goods and services. These relief measures will accelerate the emergence of green shoots in a nation's economy. These are NOT the times to increase the direct or indirect tax burden on the citizens.

> *I contend that for a nation to try to tax itself into prosperity is like a man standing in a bucket who is trying to lift himself up by the handle.*
> *- Winston S. Churchill.*

Printing unlimited and uncontrolled amounts of money is tempting, wrong and harmful and must be avoided by every nation. It is an economic suicide. Even controlled amounts of money printing shall be the very last resort by any nation.

Nations must recognize and promote digital currencies. Digital currencies must be accepted and promoted as a means of financial transactions. This will bring digital currency investments into the main stream and create revenue streams for the nations.

Amnesty schemes for black money hoarders to bring in black money into the mainstream economy are the need of the hour. Nations without exceptions have to resort to such amnesty schemes.

Release inmates from jails and decongest the prisons. Release political prisoners, human rights defendants, environmentalists, etc. Release under trials, juveniles and minor criminals (infraction and misdemeanour criminals).

The Gulf Co-operation Council (GCC) Countries:

Gulf Cooperation Council (GCC) countries (UAE, Kuwait, Bahrain, Saudi Arabia, Qatar and Oman) will need to sell assets and introduce income tax. The GCC nations are facing a double whammy. A declining demand for oil, due to alternative and green energy technologies (growing use of electric cars for example) on the one hand and the global economic impact of the pandemic that has reduced oil consumption and demand drastically on the other hand. All these new challenges come on the backdrop of already low crude prices prevailing before the onset of this pandemic due to abundance of oil in the market.

The days of an oil based economy for the GCC countries are numbered. This realization must prevail. The GCC nations must introduce income tax applicable to their citizens as well as expatriates. To begin with, I propose the following tax slabs:

Sr. No.	Annual Income Slabs	Proposed Income Tax
1	First AED 500,000	5%
2	AED 500,000 to 1 million	10%
3	AED 1 million to 5 million	20%
4	AED 5 million onwards	30%

While I have used AED (UAE currency) here, the respective figures for Qatar and Saudi Arabia could be the same in QAR and SAR respectively. Oman, Kuwait and Bahrain can work out near equivalents to the above figures for their respective currencies. Comparisons to other nations around the globe can lead to the conclusion that these proposed income tax levels are significantly lower. However these are deliberately kept lower (to make a start in these nations that have had no income tax regimes for their citizens) thus making it easier to digest for the citizens on the one hand and providing additional revenue streams to the governments on the other hand given the current grim scenario in global economy.

All GCC nations must undertake sweeping labour reforms to retain talent under these difficult times. They must end the Kafala (sponsor) system of employment, introduce minimum wages and allow switching of jobs by expatriates at the least. In the post pandemic era presenting a subdued economic scenario, the GCC nations will find it difficult to retain expatriates. A more liberal labour reform in line with international standards in the GCC countries is long overdue. The pandemic has only added to its importance.

All GCC countries must introduce a naturalization program to award citizenship to talented individuals, engineers, doctors, domain experts, academicians, scientists, research scholars, professionals and the likes without compromising on their culture and traditions. This will add to their talent pool, prevent outflow of money and help achieve self-sufficiency. This is also necessitated by the fact that 4 out of 6 GCC countries have a fertility rate below the threshold limit of 2.1 required to maintain population replacement. The fertility rates in the GCC Countries for the year 2020 as per CIA World Fact Book are as follows:

Sr.No.	GCC Country	Fertility Rate
1	Oman	2.76
2	Kuwait	2.26
3	Saudi Arabia	1.95
4	Qatar	1.88
5	UAE	1.73
6	Bahrain	1.69

There is also a need for these nations to industrialize massively with the aim of achieving self-sufficiency and reducing imports, increasing local job opportunities and promoting local level R & D thereby reducing the outflow of money.

8
The Role of Local Institutions & Individuals

I include state/provincial governments, administrations, corporates, NGO's, individuals in this category.

For the next few years, Corporate Social Responsibility (CSR) funds should be largely spent in prevention, treatment, relief and rehabilitation efforts pertaining to the pandemic and providing monetary relief to the deserving.

Development of online infrastructure and promoting work from home (WFH) culture where possible shall be prioritized.

Employers with gradually reducing budgets at hand shall consider salary reduction for their staff over job cuts as a first line of spending cuts. That will minimize job losses and ensure employees and their families are still able to cater to basic needs at the least.

> *Confronting a dangerous pandemic requires containing spread wherever it is reasonably possible. Sensible measures such as universal masking, testing and widespread and rapid contact tracing can help. The best way to protect the vulnerable is to try to protect everyone.*
> *- Scott Gottlieb*

Individuals and NGO's shall prioritize help for the needy, devoting time and effort for social work, volunteering, philanthropy, etc. They can undertake charity works and crowd funding to fulfil specific goals and targets in helping the needy.

State/Provincial governments shall provide relief in local taxes and cess for all acts and deeds aimed at providing medical relief and support to the affected. These governments need to work out local level strategies and a full set of measures to aid and undertake delivery of healthcare, aid and relief to the affected citizens.

Can't write much in this section. The realization of the gravity of the situation by all concerned is fundamental to ensuring proactive acts and deeds voluntarily to help ease the situation.

> *The worldwide response to COVID-19 has demonstrated the power of solidarity. People are spreading kindness through their words & deeds while inspiring others to do the same. No act of goodwill is too small in the fight against the pandemic.*
> *- UN*

9
Conclusion

The world faces an unprecedented and never before situation with a double assault from the pandemic and the looming economic depression. The failure of humanity to live up to the challenge could lead to a prolonged period of depression much worse than the great depression of the 1930's in scale and devastation. The stakes are high, and the need for bold, visionary leadership at the global, national and local levels is more than ever before. Unlike the last great depression, economies of the world are so intertwined in the present days that even one major economy collapsing or going into severe depression will have ripple effects across the globe.

> *What used to work for us in the past is not going to work for us going forward.*
> *- Adel Ahmad Al Redha, Emirates COO*

Humanity can still salvage the situation with unprecedented and swift actions and measures, tough and difficult decisions, revolutionary thinking, and sacrifices in the short term. Failure to do so has disastrous consequences lined up on the horizon.

> *Insanity is doing the same thing over and over again and expecting different results.*
> *- Anonymous*

Humanity is at a tipping point needing significant course correction with revolutionary thinking and matching actions on a scale never ever necessitated or witnessed before during peace times. Some of my suggestions and solutions may sound futuristic or unrealistic to conventional thinking but in terms of relevance their time is now. The world can ignore at its own peril.

> *COVID-19 has been likened to an X-ray, revealing fractures in the fragile skeleton of the societies we have built.*
> *- Antonio Guterres, UN Secretary General*

10

A Few Thoughts To Ponder

The pandemic has shown humanity the mirror in a way. It is time for humanity to introspect and become more aware, united, educated and cautious about the might and capabilities of Mother Nature. We will have to rewrite and revisit our priorities, attitudes and expectations going forward.

Consider the military might of humanity with more than 16,000 nuclear weapons, thousands of conventional bombs, thousands of fighter jets, thousands of missiles, aircraft carriers, submarines, tanks, attack helicopters, all kinds of smart weapons, millions of defence personnel, space crafts, rockets, satellite launchers, and what have you. And despite this entire arsenal, humanity is powerless in front of 5-10 grams of COVID-19 virus. Let that sink in fellows. Yeah 5-10 grams of the virus that has wiped out trillions of dollars, infected millions, killed nearly a million, rendered millions jobless, closed down millions of businesses and enterprises across the globe and the havoc continues unabated. I pity the nations that pursue nuclear weapons and increased military spending; I pity the leaders who flaunt their military might and arsenal when all it takes is a few grams of a microscopic virus to bring humanity to its knees.

Consider our achievements in biology and medical science over the centuries, our understanding of various species and micro-organisms, our knowledge of diseases, medicines, drugs, vaccines and cures. With all our expertise, we have been working day and night to find a vaccine for the COVID-19 virus for the past 9 months. Various nations, teams, research centres and labs are involved across the globe in this effort, and at the time of this writing, a reliable vaccine was yet to be found despite all these efforts. However the human body was successful in developing antibodies within days of infection and overcame the virus. Not one or two but millions of infected humans were able to successfully develop the required antibodies to overpower and outdo the virus. Mother Nature proved yet again that it can outwit the human achievements.

Humanity has come a long way with tremendous achievements to its credit that are commendable by any standards. However despite all our achievements, we still have a long way to go. Instead of harbouring any ego's and arrogance, we should feel humbled in front of Mother Nature. We need to unite as one in order to confront the increasingly difficult challenges that we face as humanity because when Mother Nature unleashes its wrath, it does not discriminate and it always prevails.

On another note, consolidation of nations is the need of our times. Borders and nations defined centuries ago are simply out dated. We inherited one mother earth. We as human beings have divided it creating borders, constraints, restrictions and differences and thereby given rise to discriminations, divisions, conflicts, challenges, sufferings, wars, etc. Its time most of these fake boundaries and borders are erased and the otherization (us and them) among fellow human beings are curtailed. The European Union is a good example in recent times in this regards albeit with certain limitations, but nevertheless a good starting point. We need many more such unions to begin with. At a minimum a consolidated union of nations shall have one union passport for all its citizens, one flag, one single currency of the union, one single defence force, and free movement of goods and people within the union without any border checks, customs duty, import/export tariffs and the likes. With about 200 nations doting the globe, it would be a big achievement if we can consolidate these into 20 unions by 2030-2035 and virtually into a single global village by 2050 thus eliminating the need for passports, visas, border posts, customs & import/export tariffs, armies, multiple currencies and nationalities. The humongous saving resulting thereof can be put to more productive use and benefit of mankind.

Geography has made us neighbours.
History has made us friends.
Economics has made us partners,
and necessity has made us allies.
Those whom God has so joined together,
let no man put asunder
- John F Kennedy

The pandemic has exposed humanity in many ways.

It's an eye opener for all of us.

Wake up humanity.

Be one.

11

Quote UnQuote

The pandemic has been such an awful time for so many people around the world, but it has also been a reminder for us about the things that really matter - the people in our lives and the love we have for them.
- Ananya Birla

The worst pandemic in modern history was the Spanish flu of 1918, which killed tens of millions of people. Today, with how interconnected the world is, it would spread faster.
- Bill Gates.

The COVID-19 pandemic has demonstrated that infectious diseases know no borders.
- Abigail Spanberger.

There were good-faith reasons to resort to extraordinary measures when confronting an unknown global pandemic. Most of us consented to the lockdown, even if reluctantly. However, that consent - freely given as an act of social solidarity - was not intended as a green light to giving up hard-won liberties, or a perpetual suspension of free society.
- Claire Fox

I think everyone must practice yoga, especially during this time of COVID-19 pandemic to decrease stress and anxiety. It not only helps our physical health but also helps in maintaining a good mental health.
- Jasmin Bhasin

Especially amid the COVID-19 pandemic, which has disproportionately impacted tribal communities, we must invest in infrastructure in order to advance economic recovery and create much-needed jobs.
- Sharice Davids

For a pandemic of moderate severity, this is one of our greatest challenges: helping people to understand when they do not need to worry, and when they do need to seek urgent care.
- Margaret Chan

The greatest generation was formed first by the Great Depression. They shared everything - meals, jobs, clothing.
- Tom Brokaw

The 24% unemployment reached at the depths of the Great Depression was no picnic.
- Barry Eichengreen

The Great Depression, like most other periods of severe unemployment, was produced by government mismanagement rather than by any inherent instability of the private economy.
- Milton Friedman

NOTES

....

....

....

....

....

....

....

....

....

....

....

....

....

NOTES

....

....

....

....

....

....

....

....

....

....

....

....

....

www.ingramcontent.com/pod-product-compliance
Ingram Content Group UK Ltd.
Pitfield, Milton Keynes, MK11 3LW, UK
UKHW041822200726
13854UKWH00001BA/436

9 789390 566501